BOOKWORMS

Safe Kids
Water Safety

Niños seguros
Seguridad en el agua

Dana Meachen Rau

 Marshall Cavendish
Benchmark
New York

Splash!

Water feels good on a hot day.

———————❖———————

¡Paf!

El agua es deliciosa en un día caluroso.

You need to be safe in water.

A grown-up should always be with you.

———————❖———————

Necesitas estar seguro en el agua.

Un adulto debe estar contigo siempre.

Swim where you can stand.

Do not go too deep.

———◆———

Nada donde puedas estar de pie.

No vayas a lo profundo.

Swim near a *lifeguard*.

Lifeguards keep swimmers safe.

———◆———

Nada cerca de un *salvavidas*.

Los salvavidas mantienen seguros a los nadadores.

Always swim with a buddy.

A buddy can call for help.

———————❖———————

Nada siempre con un compañero.

Un compañero puede pedir ayuda.

Never push someone in or under the water.

Never play rough in water.

———◆———

Nunca empujes a alguien al agua ni lo hundas.

Nunca juegues con brusquedad en el agua.

Do not dive in *shallow* water.

You could hit your head on the bottom.

———————❖———————

No te zambullas en agua *poco profunda*.

Podrías golpearte la cabeza en el fondo.

Watch for other swimmers when you jump.

You could hit someone in a crowded pool.

———————◆———————

Mira si hay otros nadadores cuando saltes.

Podrías golpear a alguien en una piscina llena de personas.

Beaches can have strong *waves*.

Waves can pull you under or out to sea.

———————◆———————

Las playas pueden tener *olas* fuertes.

Las olas pueden hundirte o arrastrarte mar adentro.

Blow-up toys are fun in water.

But they do not keep you safe.

———————◆———————

Los juguetes inflables son divertidos en el agua.

Pero no te mantienen seguro.

Only a *life jacket* keeps you safe.

Always wear one in a boat.

———————◆———————

Sólo un *chaleco salvavidas* te mantiene seguro.

Usa uno siempre que estés en una embarcación.

Get out of the water if there is a storm.

Lightning can hurt you in the water.

———❖———

Sal del agua si hay una tormenta.

Los rayos pueden hacerte daño en el agua.

Be a safe kid in water.

———————◆———————

Sé un niño seguro en el agua.

Be Safe
Estar seguro

buddy
compañero

life jacket
chaleco salvavidas

lifeguard
salvavidas

pool
piscina

28

storm
tormenta

waves
olas

Challenge Words

lifeguard A person who keeps swimmers safe.

life jacket A vest that helps people float.

shallow Not deep.

waves Bumps of moving water.

Palabras avanzadas

chaleco salvavidas Chaleco que ayuda que las personas floten.

olas Saltos del agua en movimiento.

poco profunda Que no es honda.

salvavidas Persona que mantiene seguros a los nadadores.

Index

Índice

About the Author

Dana Meachen Rau is the author of many other titles in the Bookworms series, as well as other nonfiction and early reader books. She lives in Burlington, Connecticut, with her husband and two children.

Sobre la autora

Dana Meachen Rau es la autora de muchos libros de la serie Bookworms y de otros libros de no ficción y de lectura para principiantes. Vive en Burlington, Connecticut, con su esposo y sus dos hijos.

With thanks to the Reading Consultants:

Nanci Vargus, Ed.D., is an Assistant Professor of Elementary Education at the University of Indianapolis.

Beth Walker Gambro is an Adjunct Professor at the University of Saint Francis in Joliet, Illinois.

Agradecemos a las asesoras de lectura:

Nanci Vargus, doctora en Educación, es profesora auxiliar de Educación Primaria en la Universidad de Indianápolis.

Beth Walker Gambro es profesora adjunta en la Universidad de Saint Francis en Joliet, Illinois.

Marshall Cavendish Benchmark
99 White Plains Road
Tarrytown, New York 10591
www.marshallcavendish.us

Library of Congress Cataloging-in-Publication Data

Rau, Dana Meachen, 1971–
[Water safety. English & Spanish]
Water safety = Seguridad en el agua / Dana Meachen Rau.
p. cm. — (Bookworms. Safe kids = Niños seguros)
Includes index.
Parallel text in English and Spanish; translated from the English.
ISBN 978-0-7614-4779-5 (bilingual ed.) — ISBN 978-0-7614-4088-8 (English ed.)
1. Aquatic sports—Safety measures—Juvenile literature. I. Title. II. Title: Seguridad en el agua.
GV770.6R37513 2009
797.2—dc22
2009016338

Editor: Christina Gardeski
Publisher: Michelle Bisson
Designer: Virginia Pope
Art Director: Anahid Hamparian

Spanish Translation and Text Composition by Victory Productions, Inc.
www.victoryprd.com

Photo Research by Anne Burns Images

Cover Photo by *Alamy Images*/Chuck Franklin

The photographs in this book are used with permission and through the courtesy of:
Corbis: pp. 1, 11, 28TL Fabio Cardoso/zefa; p. 3 Kiyotaka Kitajima; pp. 19, 29R Flynn Larsen/zefa;
pp. 23, 28TR Tony Demin; p. 25, 29L Jim Reed. *Alamy Images*: p. 5 Craig Lovell/Eagle Visions Photography;
p. 7 Ben Ramos. *SuperStock*: pp. 9, 28BL age fotostock. *Getty*: pp. 13, 27 Dorgie Productions;
p. 15 Grant Symon; pp. 17, 28BR Joos Mind; p. 21 Gary Chapman.

Printed in Malaysia
1 3 5 6 4 2